AF473649

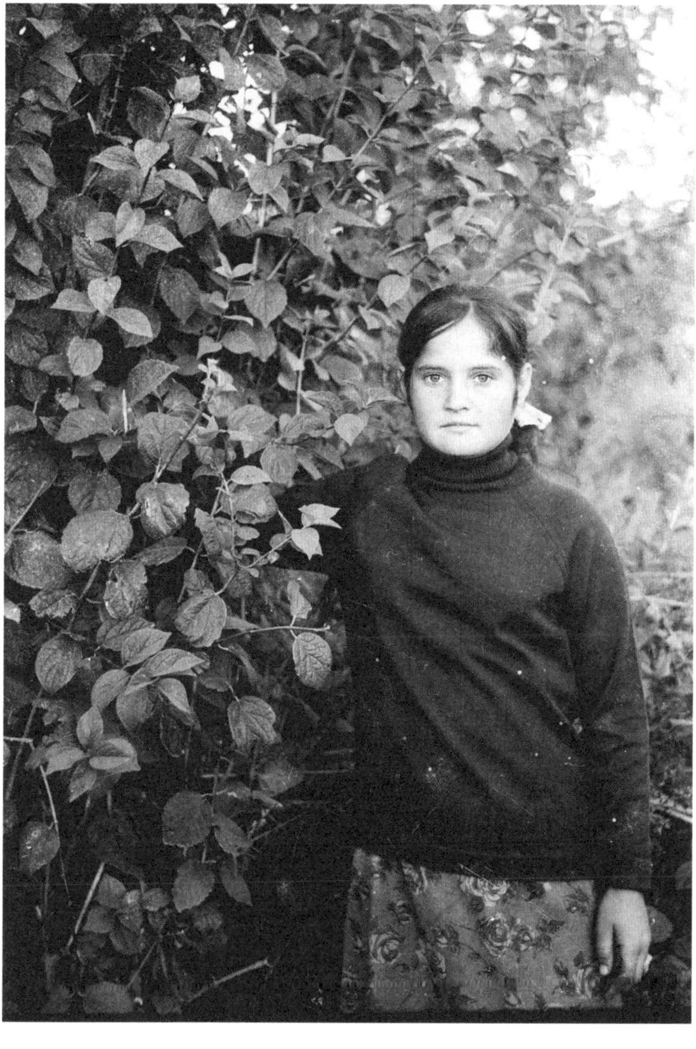

Es war einmal in Moldawien

Die Fotografien von Vasilii Lefter (1943–1982) wurden zu seinen Lebzeiten nie veröffentlicht. Dabei war es sein Traum, als Fotograf oder Künstler ernst genommen und international ausgestellt oder veröffentlicht zu werden. Fünfundzwanzig Jahre lagen die Bilder in staubigen Schachteln auf dem Balkon der elterlichen Wohnung in Chișinău, der Hauptstadt Moldawiens, als seine Tochter, die Künstlerin Tatiana Fiodorova (* 1976) sie entdeckte. Lefter hinterließ eine Kiev-Kamera und unzählige kleine Fotografien, Negative, Filmrollen, Zeichnungen und Gemälde, aber auch Dinge wie eine Schachtel mit handgearbeiteten kyrillischen Buchstaben und ein selbst fotoreproduziertes sowjetisches Buch über Heilpflanzen sowie Schablonen und Zeichnungen für die Propagandaplakate, die er als freier Gestalter – einer Position, die es im kommunistischen Moldawien eigentlich nicht geben konnte – für die Kolchosen der Umgebung entwarf und malte. Für diese freie, aber völlig unsichere Existenz gab er seinen systemkonformen aber unbefriedigenden Bürojob im Bauministerium auf, wo er ab 1970 angestellt war. Lefter war Autodidakt und hatte sich sein Wissen mithilfe von Fotobüchern angeeignet, fotografierte ausschließlich schwarzweiß und entwickelte seine kleinformatigen Bilder im heimischen Badezimmer. Einen Großteil des ohnehin bescheidenen Einkommens gab er für seine fotografische Leidenschaft sowie für Bücher, Leinwände und Farben aus. Der Erwerb eines Motorrollers belastete die dadurch schon stark beanspruchte Haushaltskasse zusätzlich. Häufig verbrachte er die Wochenenden auf dem Land um Chișinău, wo er die Dorfbewohner in ihren Gärten, bei Hochzeiten, im Wald oder in Versammlungsräumen porträtierte. Familienmitglieder posierten vor seiner Kamera, häufig als Paare. Die in seinen Bildern wiederholt abgebildeten Babies und Statussymbole wie Kofferradios wurden als Requisiten unter der Porträtierten weitergereicht. Die oft identischen Kleider zeugen von der Vielfalt kommunistischer Einheitsmode. Doch seine Sichtweise des Alltags im sowjetischen Moldawien entsprach nicht den offiziell verordneten Inhalten und Bildern, weshalb er auch keine Aufnahme in den Künstlerverband Moldawiens fand – damals die Voraussetzung, um ausgestellt oder publiziert zu werden. Jetzt, 36 Jahre nach seinem Tod und 28 Jahre nach Fall des Eisernen Vorhangs, werden die Fotografien von Vasilii Lefter erstmals international veröffentlicht und ausgestellt – sein Traum wird wahr.

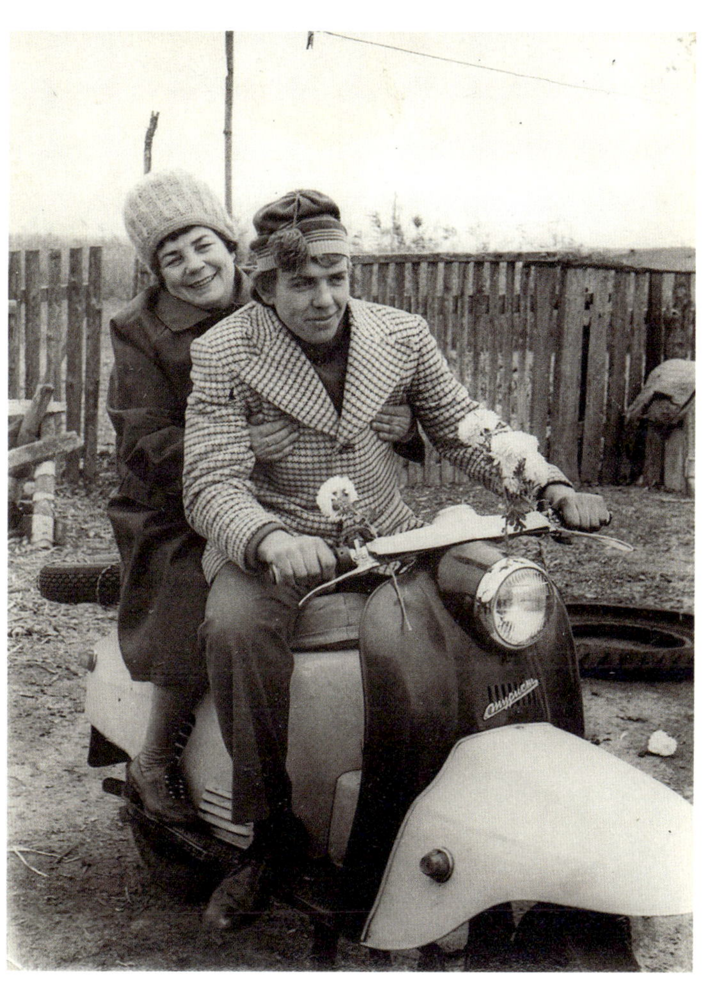

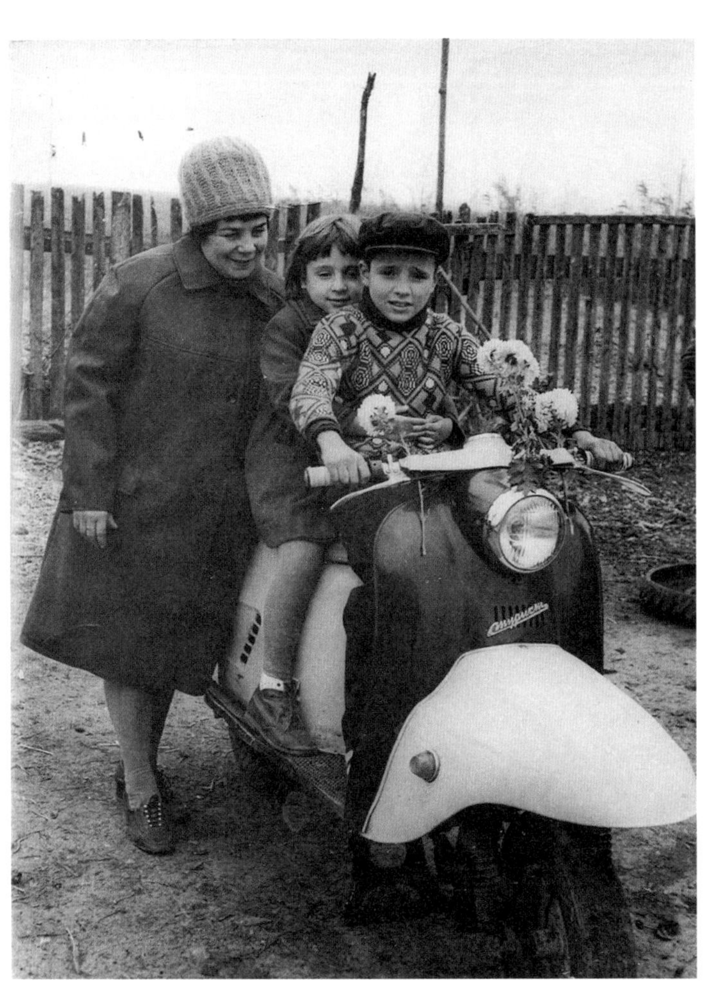

Once Upon a Time in Moldavia

The photographs of Vasilii Lefter (1943–1982) were never published during his lifetime. Yet it was always his dream to be taken seriously as a photographer or artist and to have international exhibitions and publications. When his daughter, the artist Tatiana Fiodorova (born in 1976), discovered them, the boxed images had been gathering dust for twenty-five years on the balcony of her parents' apartment in Chișinău, the capital of Moldavia. Lefter left behind a Kiev camera and countless small-format photographs, negatives, rolls of film, drawings and paintings, and also things like a box with handmade Cyrillic letters, a reproduction of a Soviet book on medicinal herbs, and stencils and drawings for the propaganda posters that he had designed and painted as a freelance graphic designer—a position that could not really exist in Communist Moldavia—for the kolkhozes of the region. He gave up his conformist but unsatisfying desk job at the Ministry of Building, where he had been employed since 1970, for this free but totally insecure existence. Lefter was self-taught and had accumulated his knowledge from photography books; his photographs were black and white, and he developed his small-format pictures in his bathroom at home. He spent a large portion of his meager earnings on his passion for photography, as well as books, canvases, and paints. His budget was further strained when he bought a motor scooter. He often spent weekends in the countryside around Chișinău, where he photographed the villagers in their gardens, at weddings, in the forest, or in community rooms. Family members posed for his camera, often as couples. Babies and status symbols such as portable radios, which often reappear in his pictures, were often shared by the sitters as props. The often identical clothing bears witness to the uniformity of Communist fashion. Yet his view of everyday life in Soviet Moldavia did not correspond with the officially prescribed content for images, which is why none of his pictures were accepted by the artist association of Moldavia—back then that was the one requirement for mounting an exhibition or publishing. Now, thirty-six years after his death and twenty-eight years after the fall of the Iron Curtain, the photographs are being shown for the first time in an international exhibition—the fulfilment of his dream.

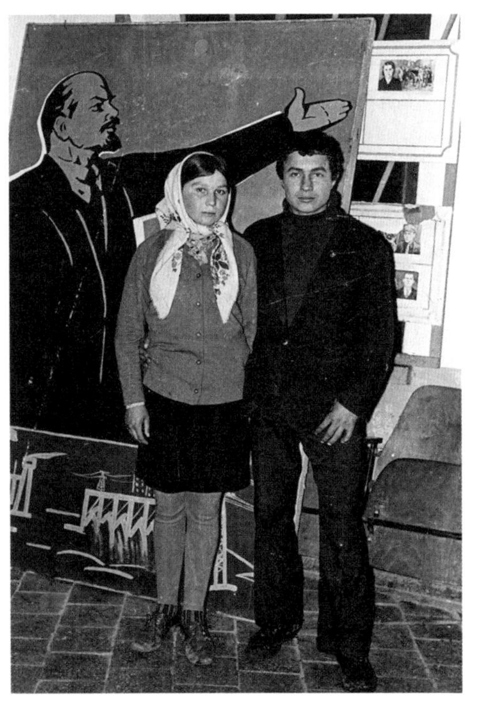

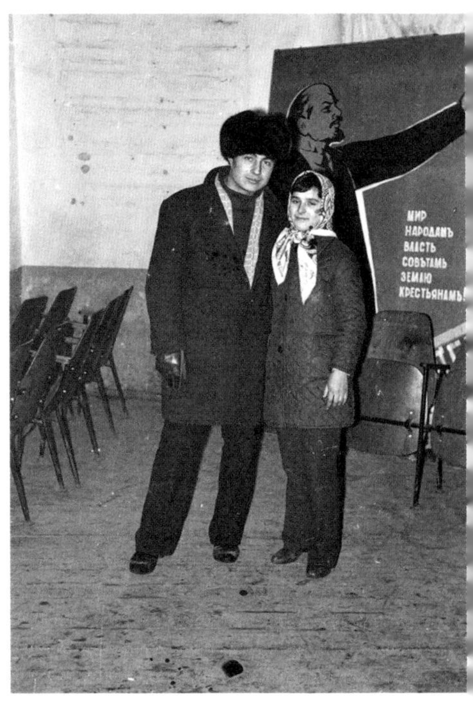
МИР
НАРОДАМЪ
ВЛАСТЬ
СОВѢТАМЬ
ЗЕМЛЮ
КРЕСТЬЯНАМЪ!

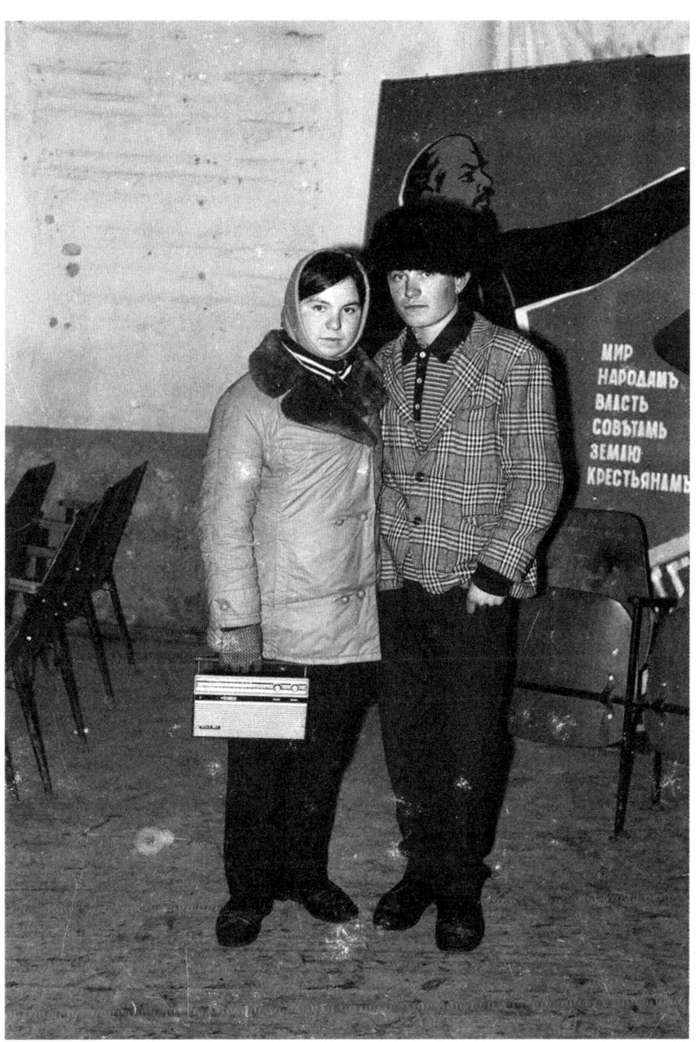
МИР
НАРОДАМЪ
ВЛАСТЬ
СОВѢТАМЪ
ЗЕМЛЮ
КРЕСТЬЯНАМ

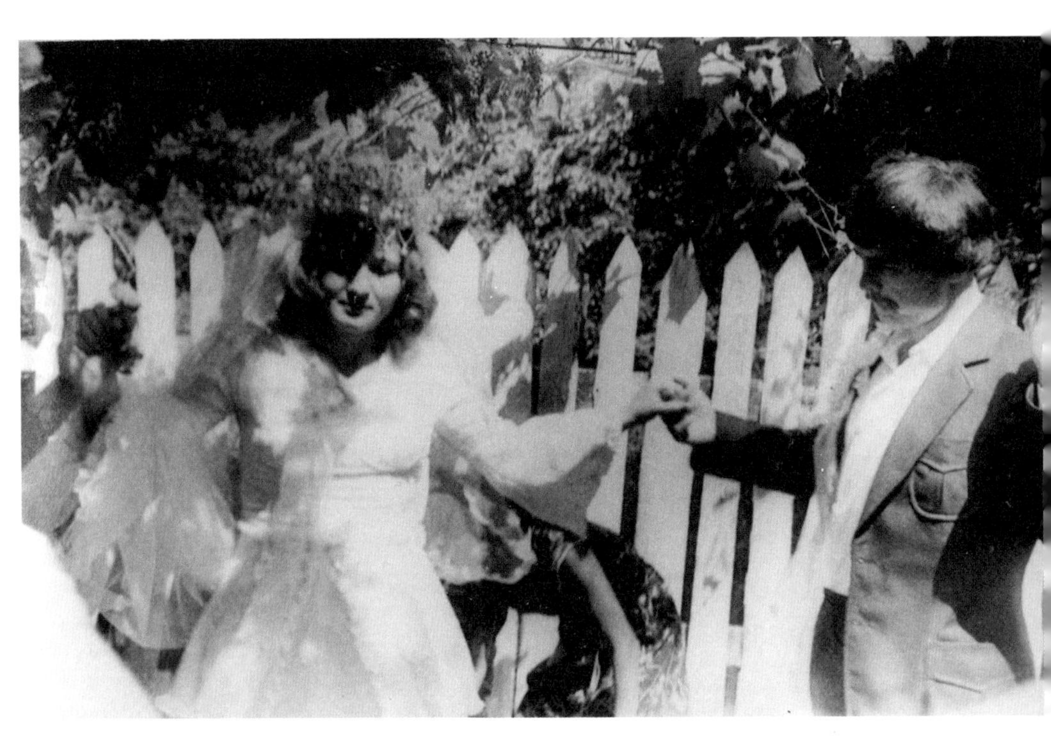

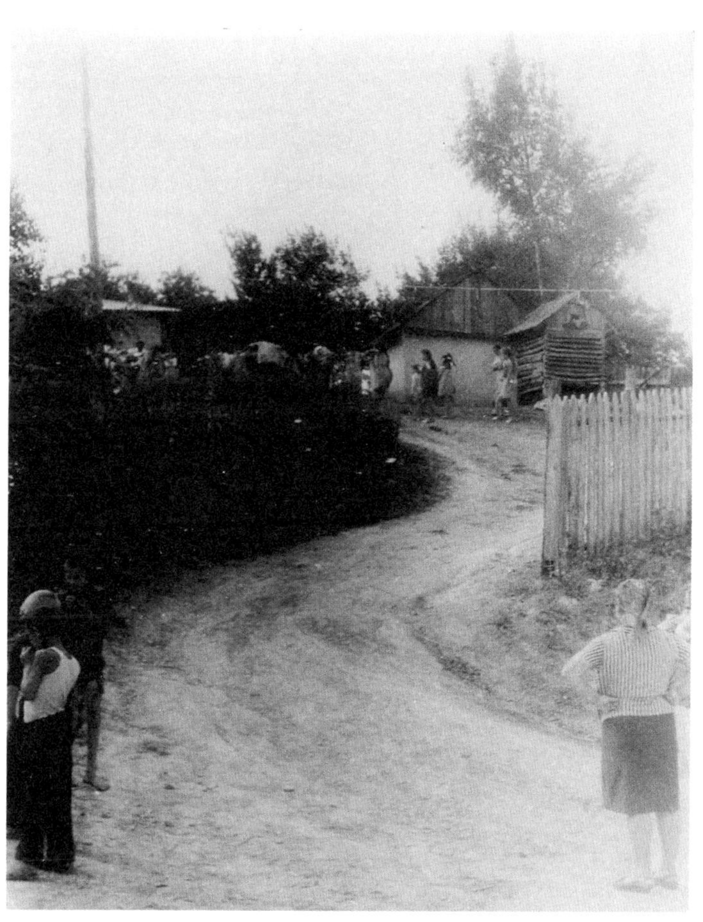

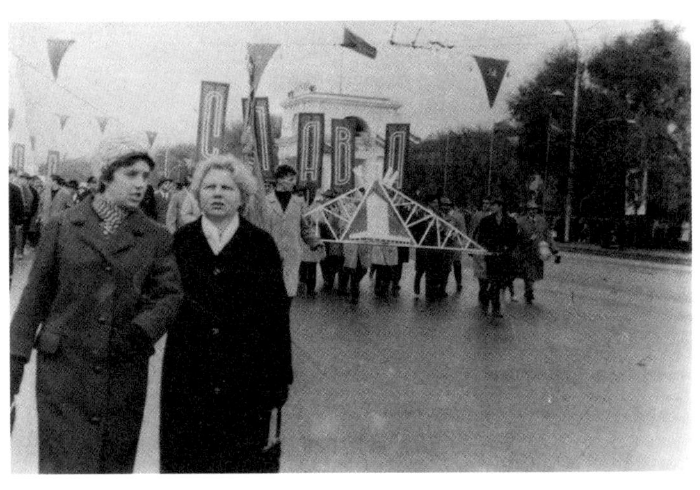

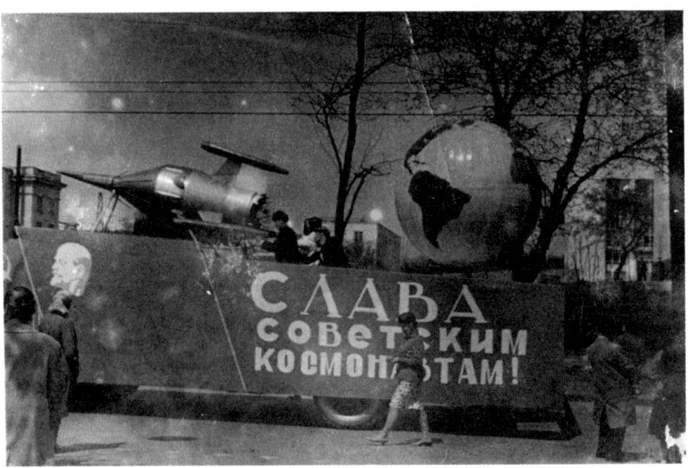
СЛАВА

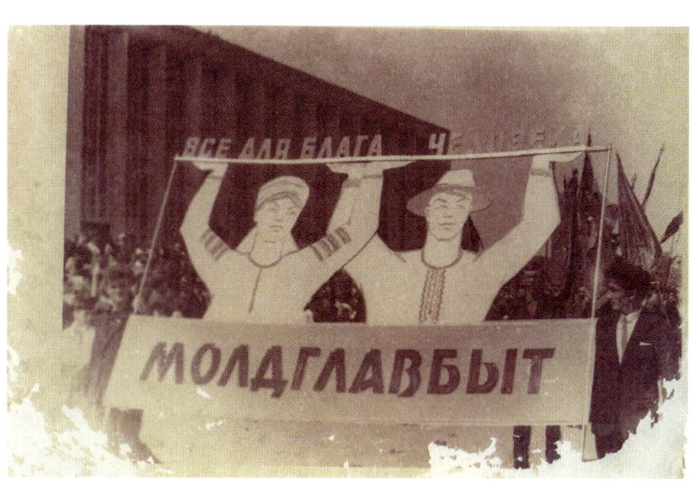
ВСЕ ДЛЯ БЛАГА
МОЛДГЛАВБЫТ

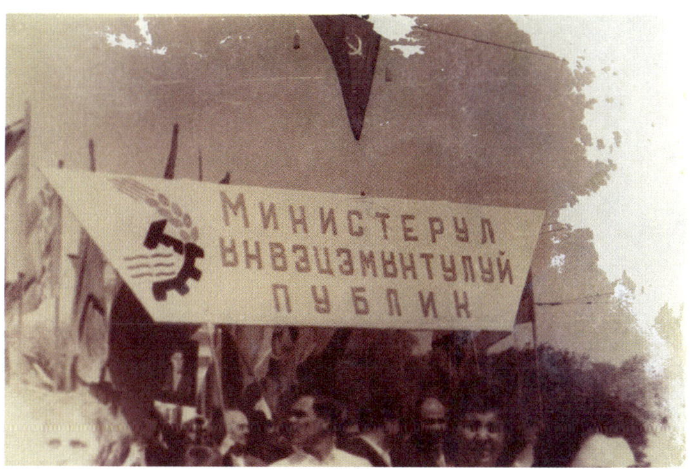
МИНИСТЕРУЛ
ИНВЭЦЭМЫНТУЛУЙ
ПУБЛИК

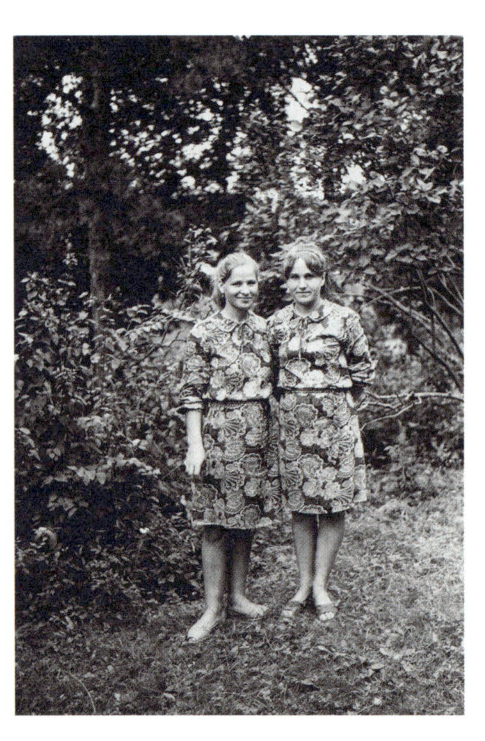

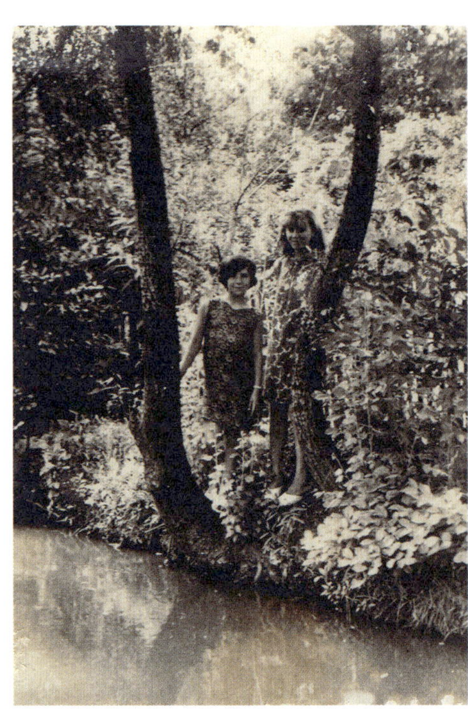

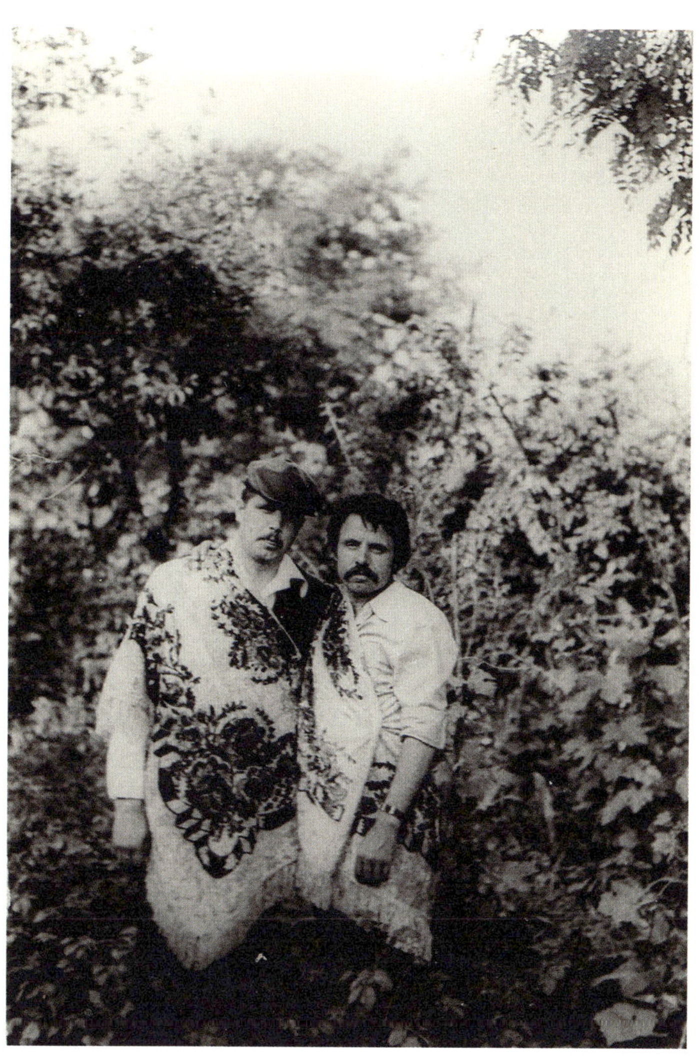

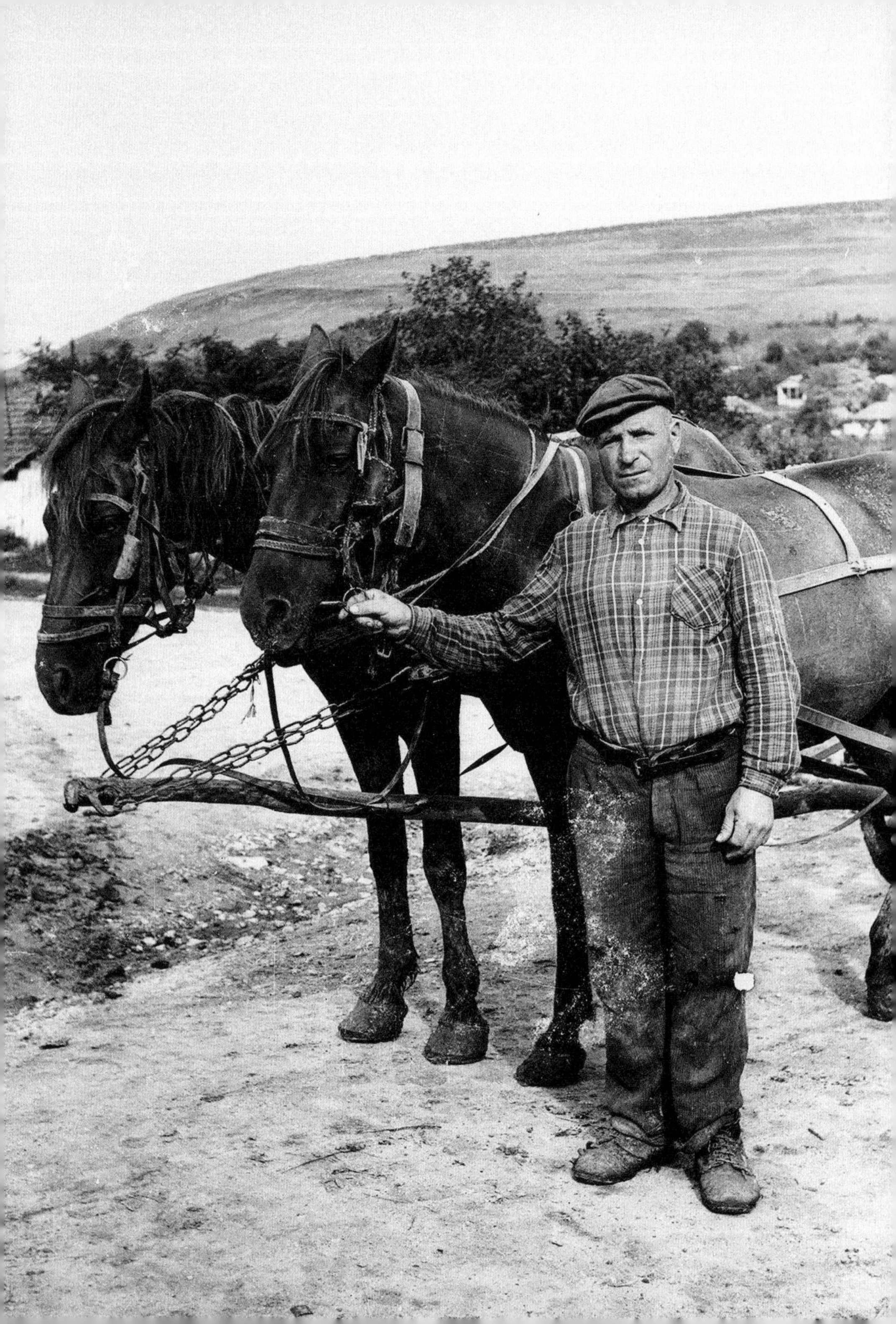

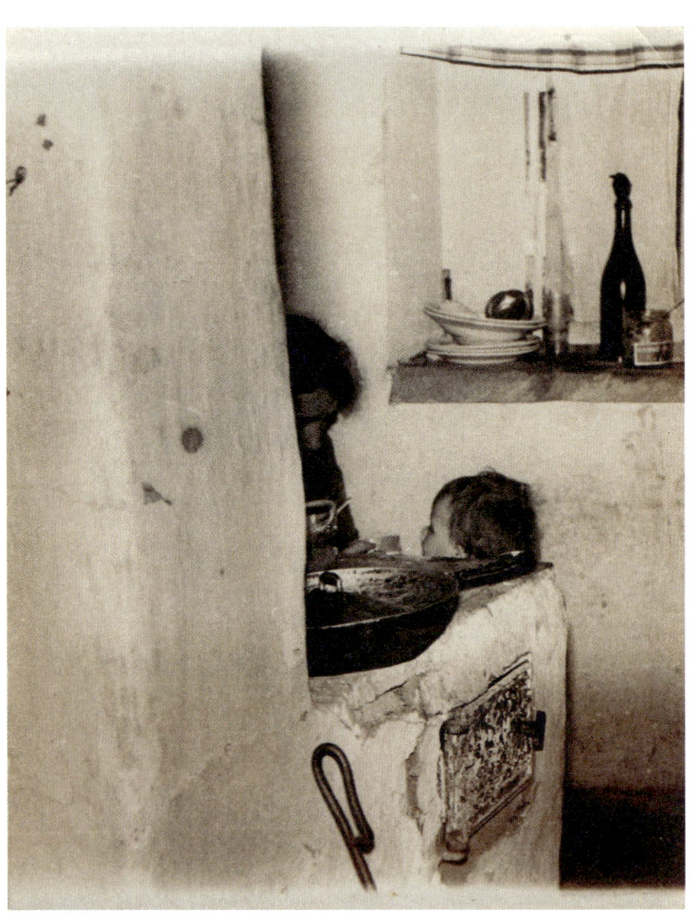

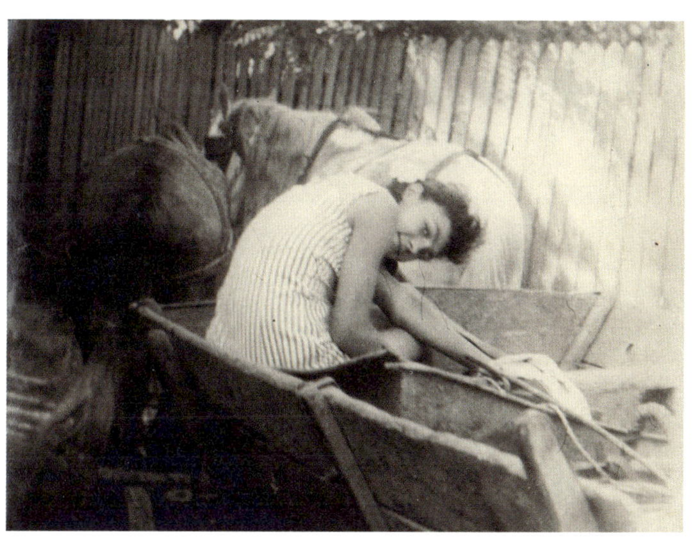

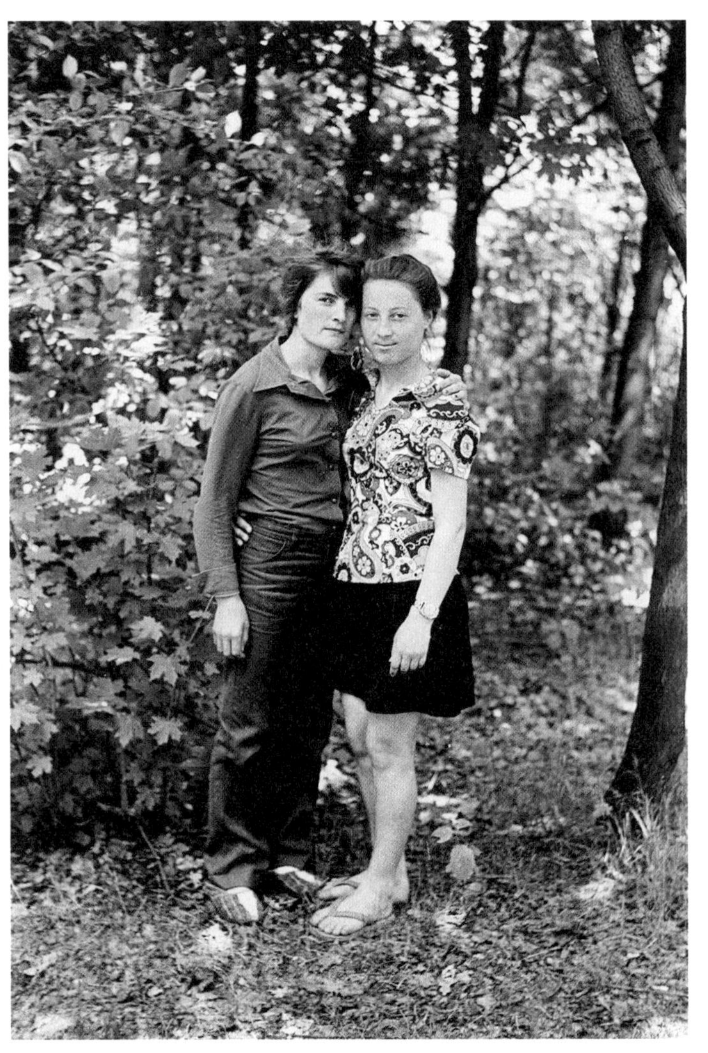

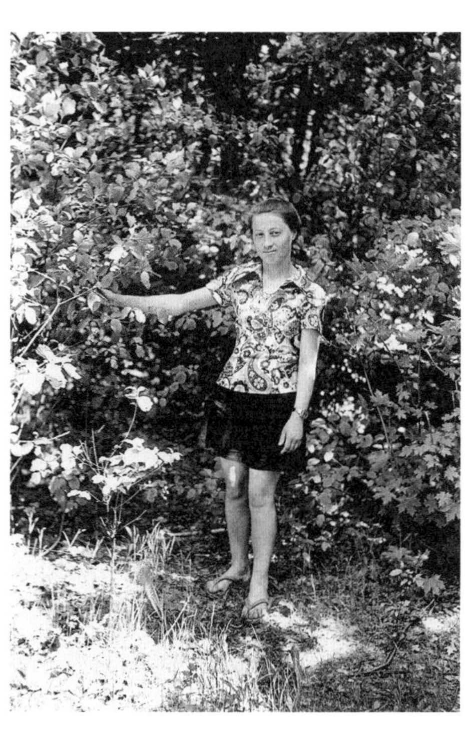
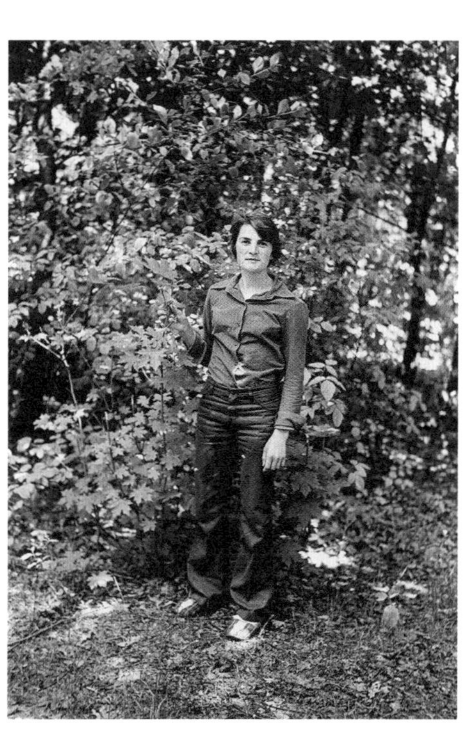

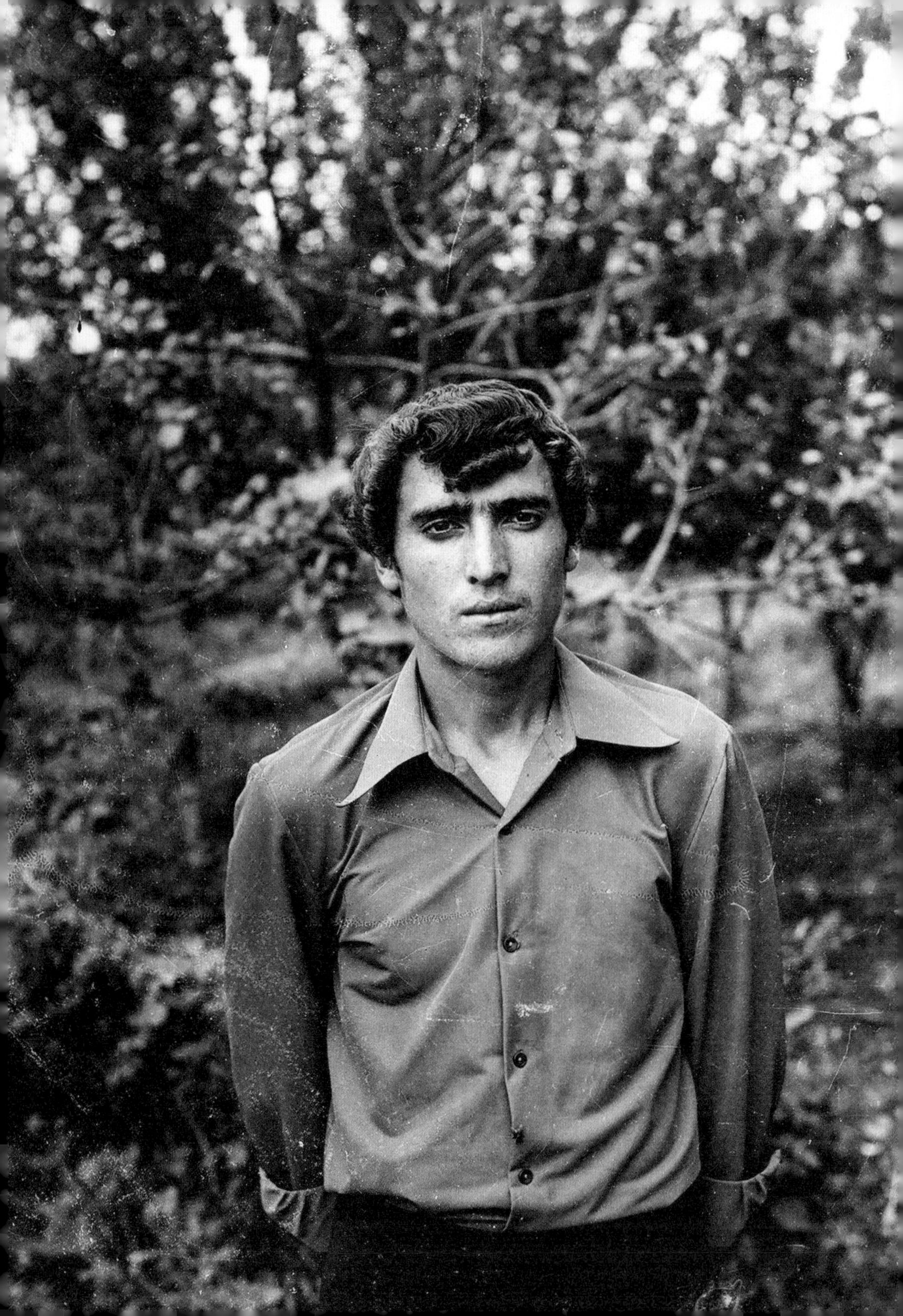

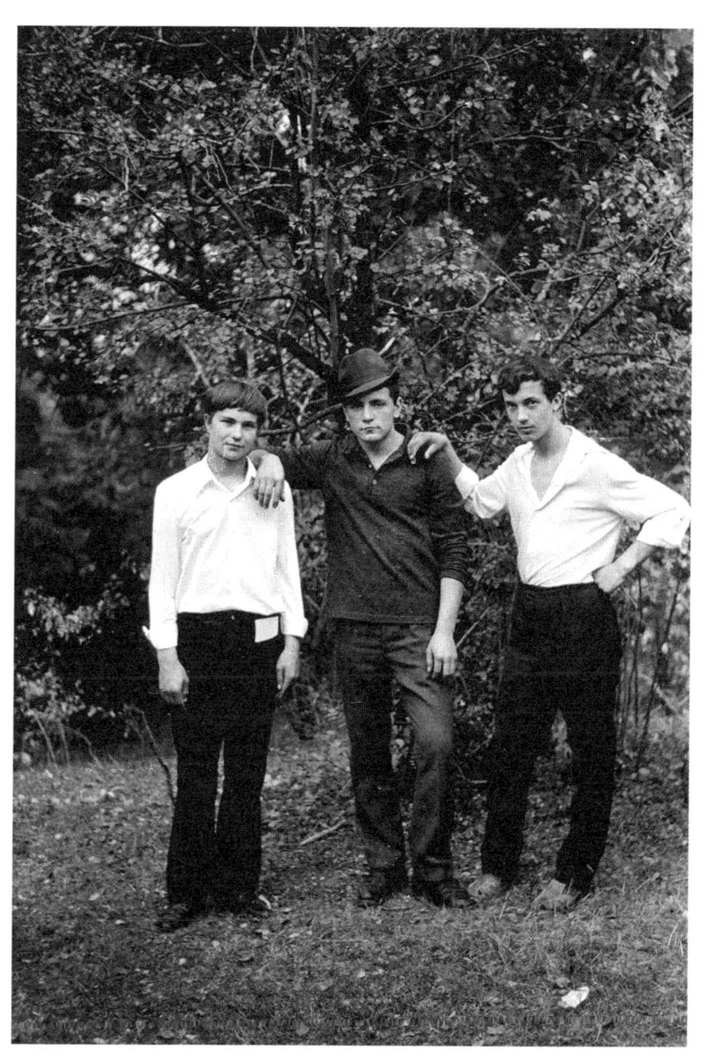

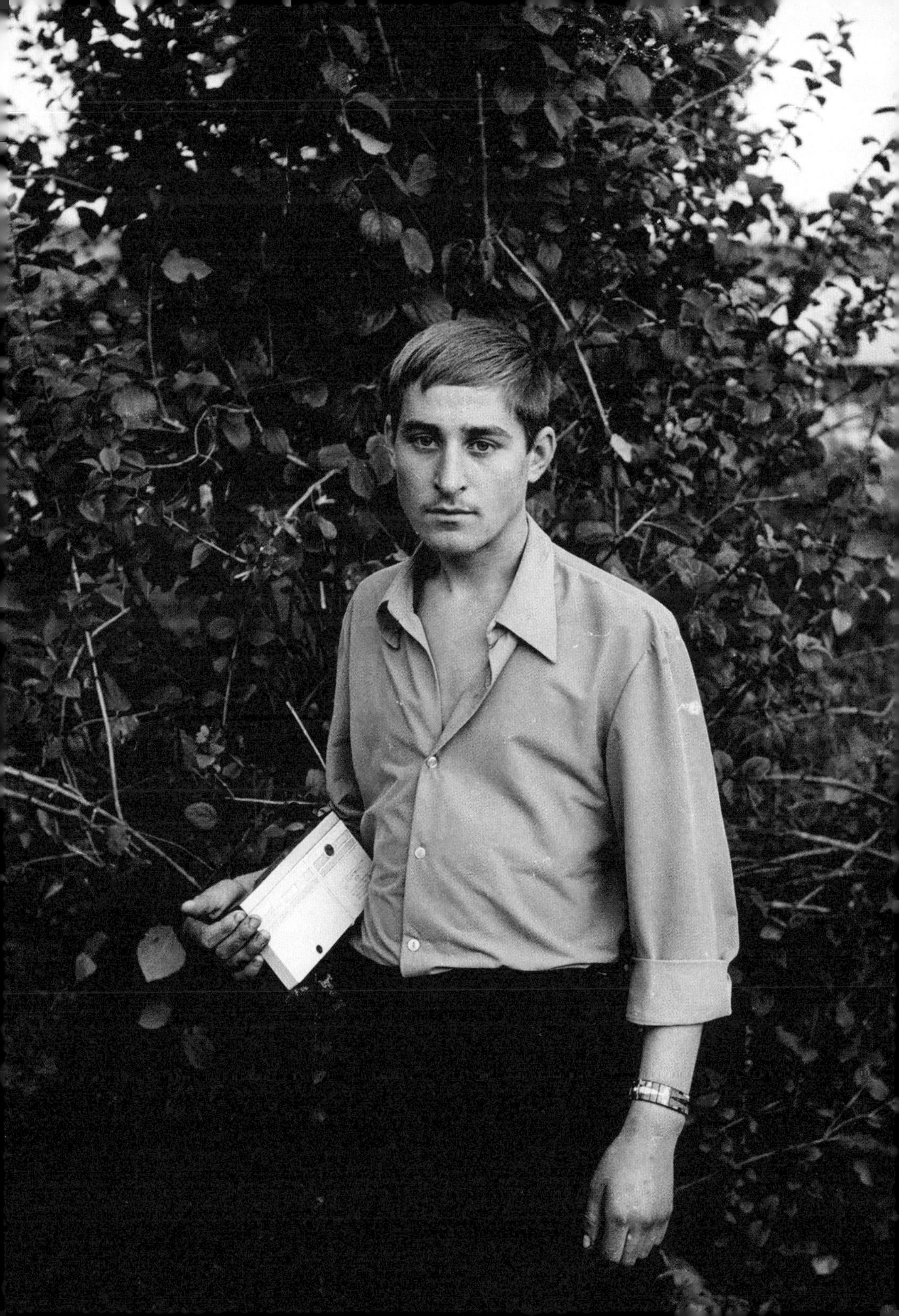

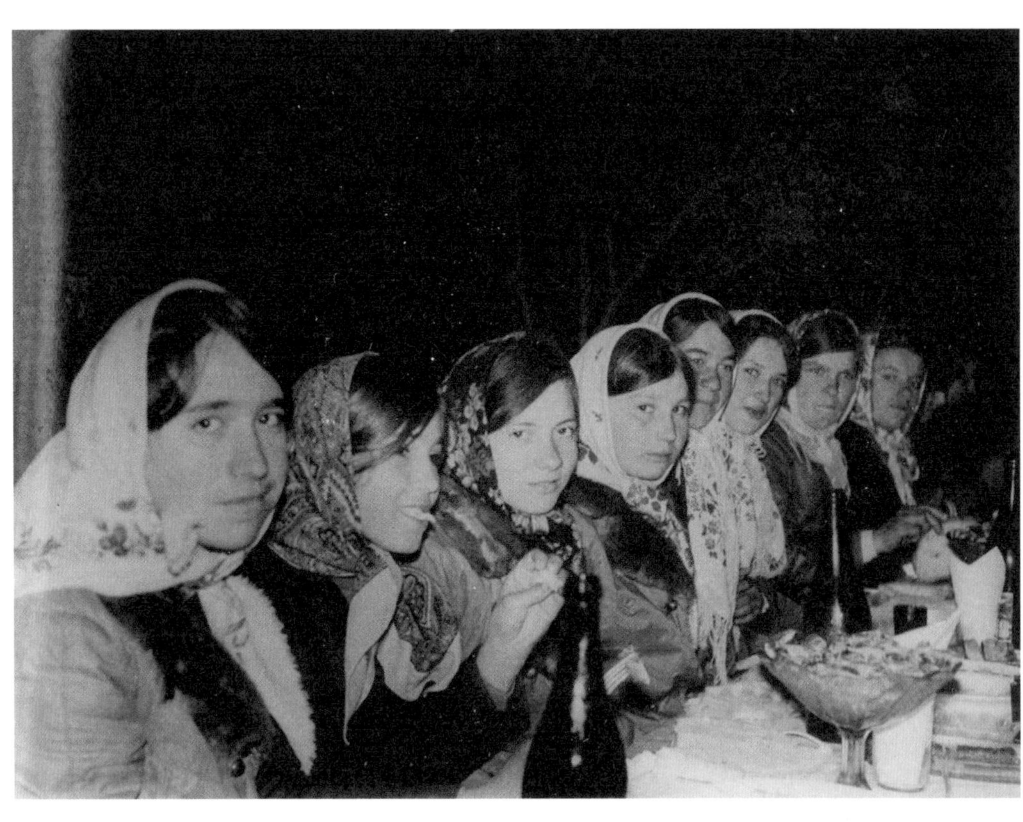

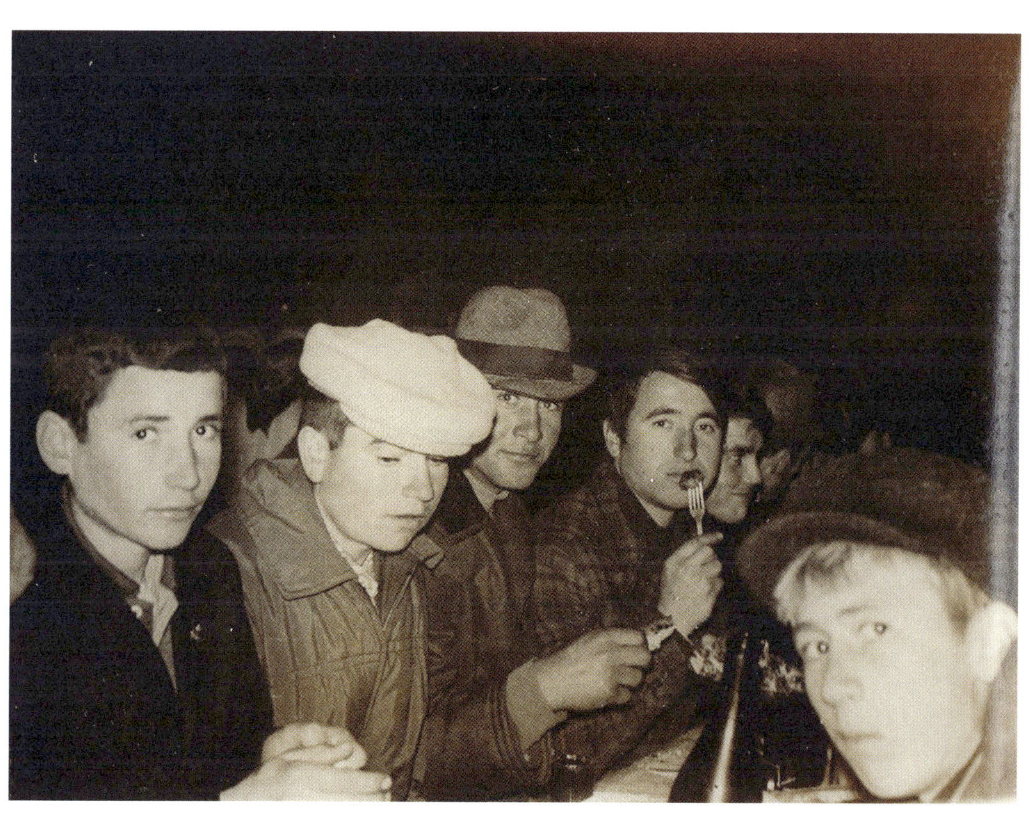

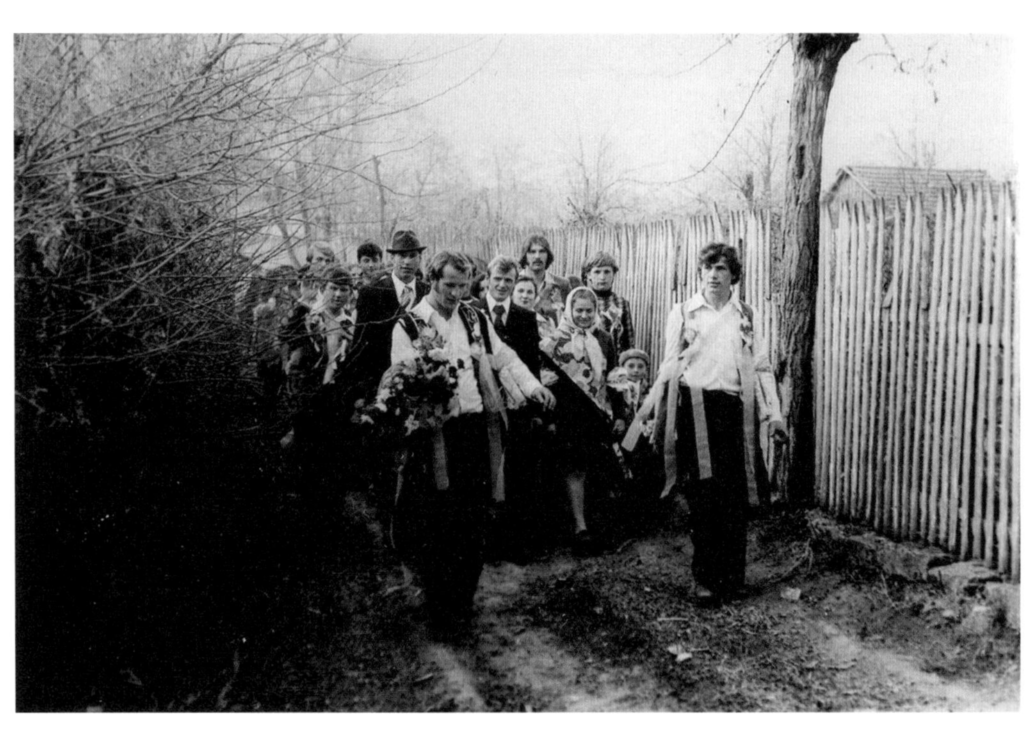

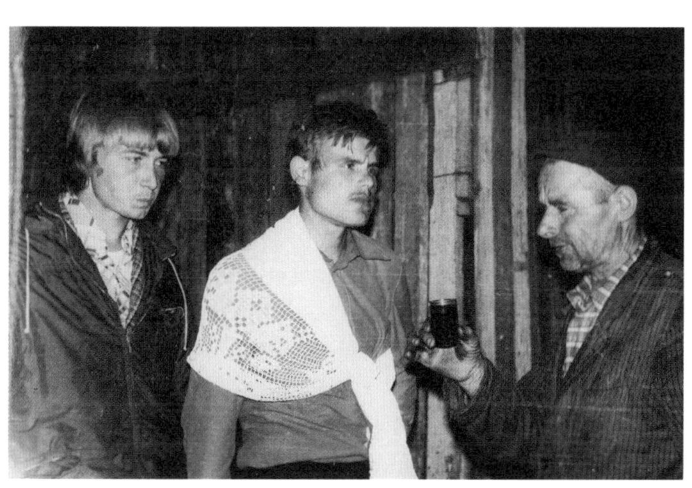

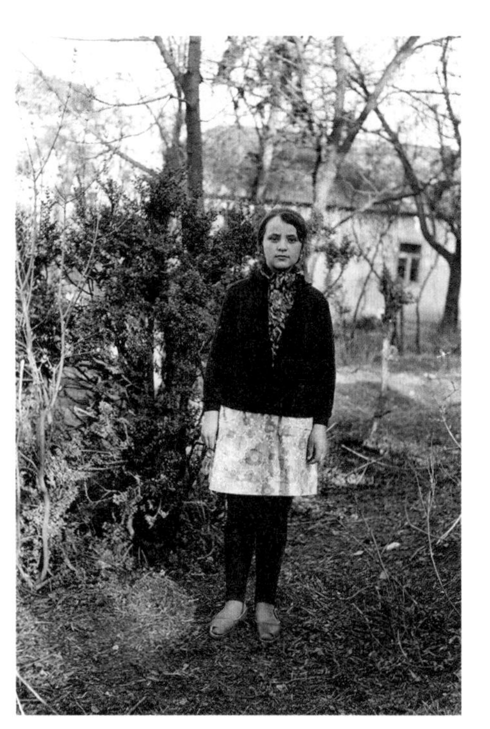

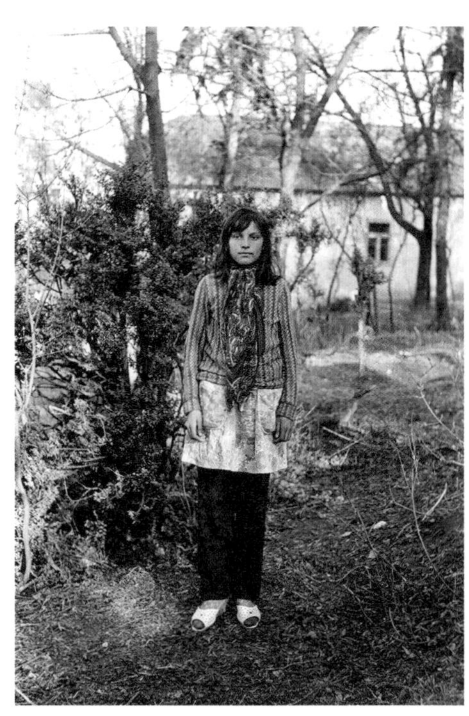

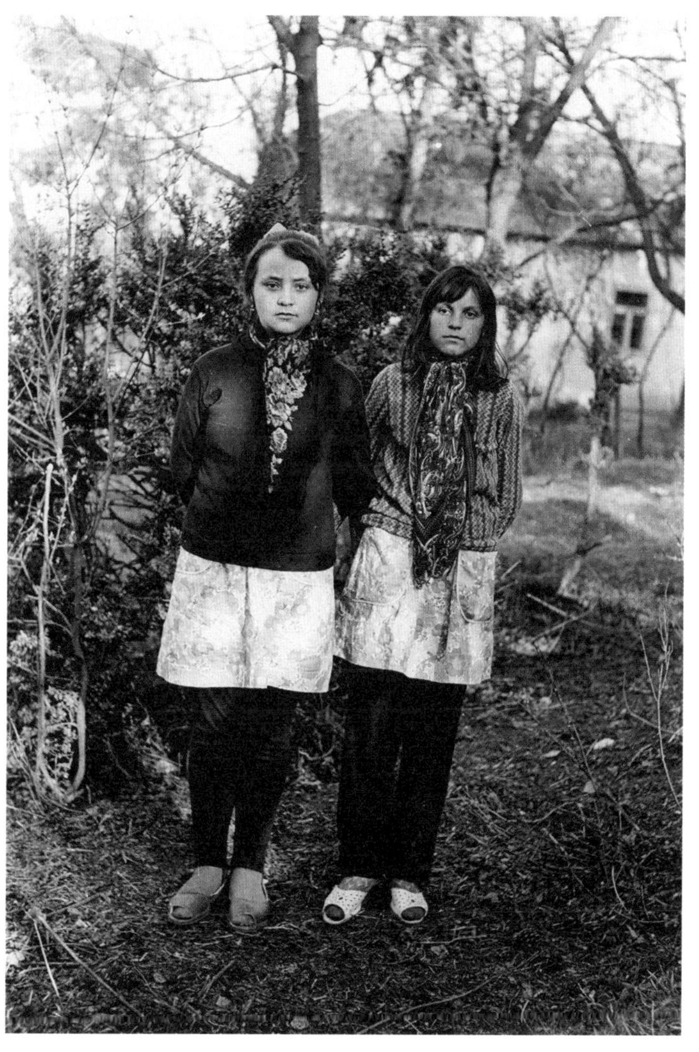

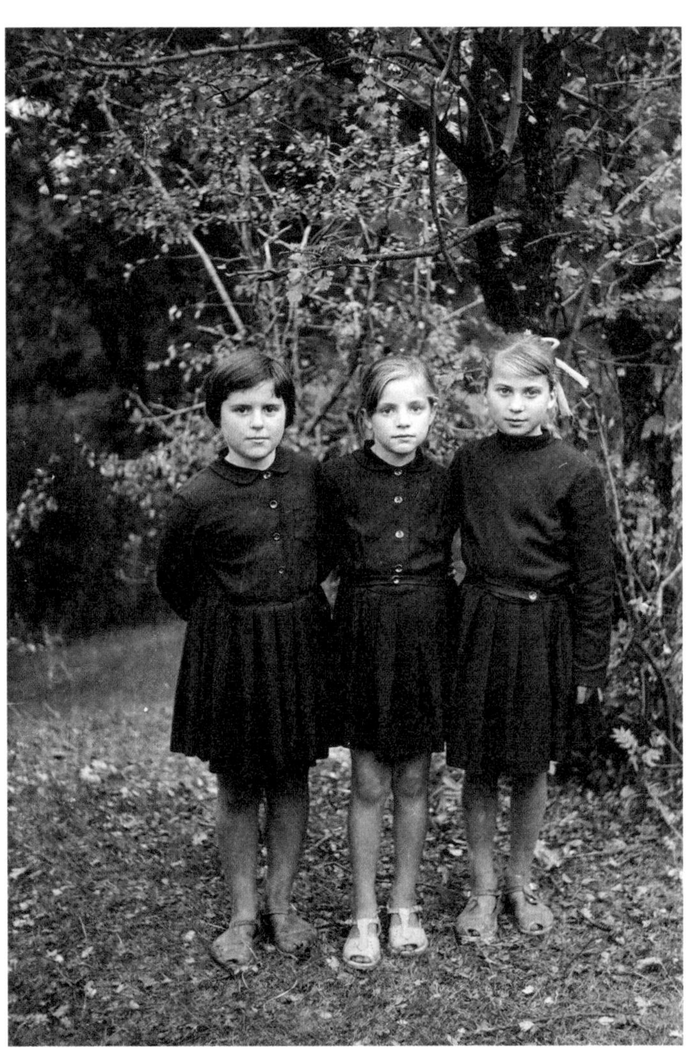

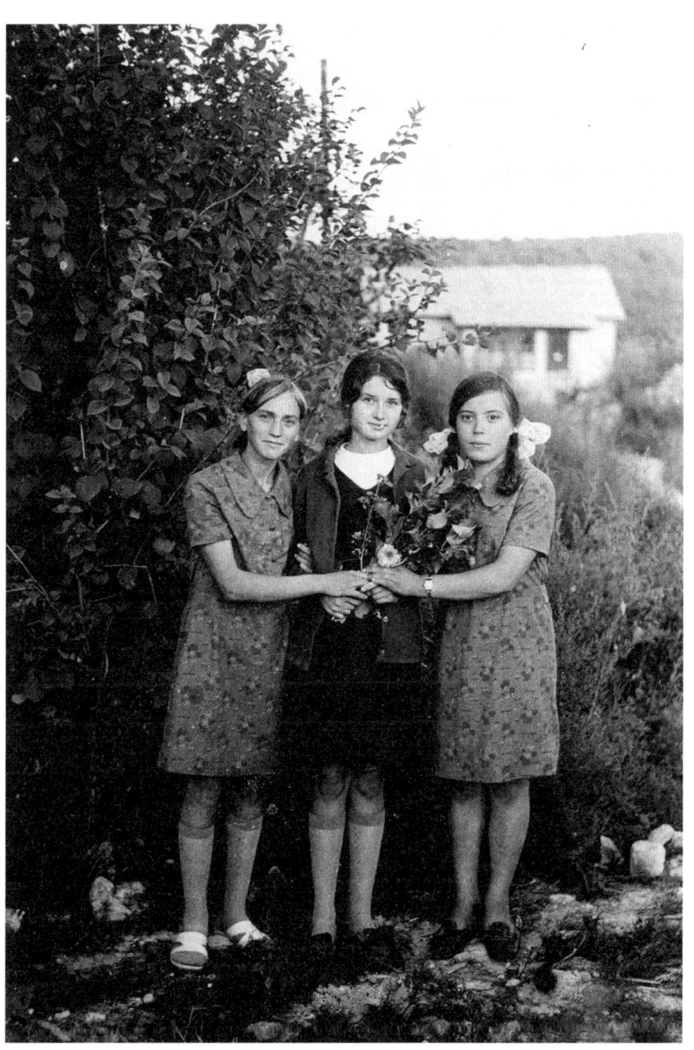

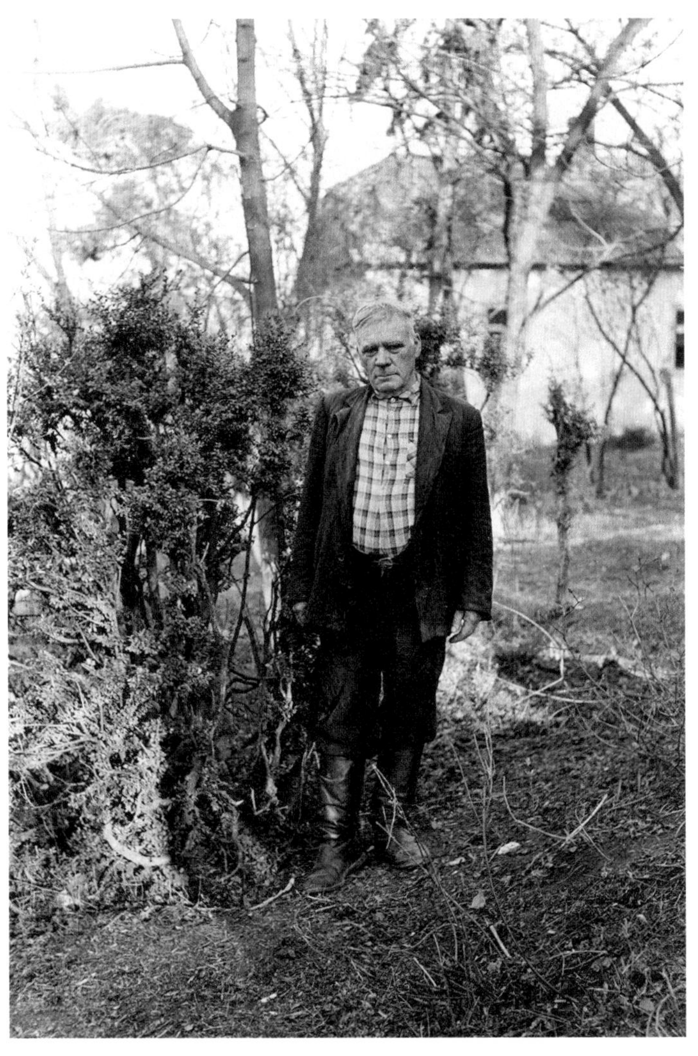

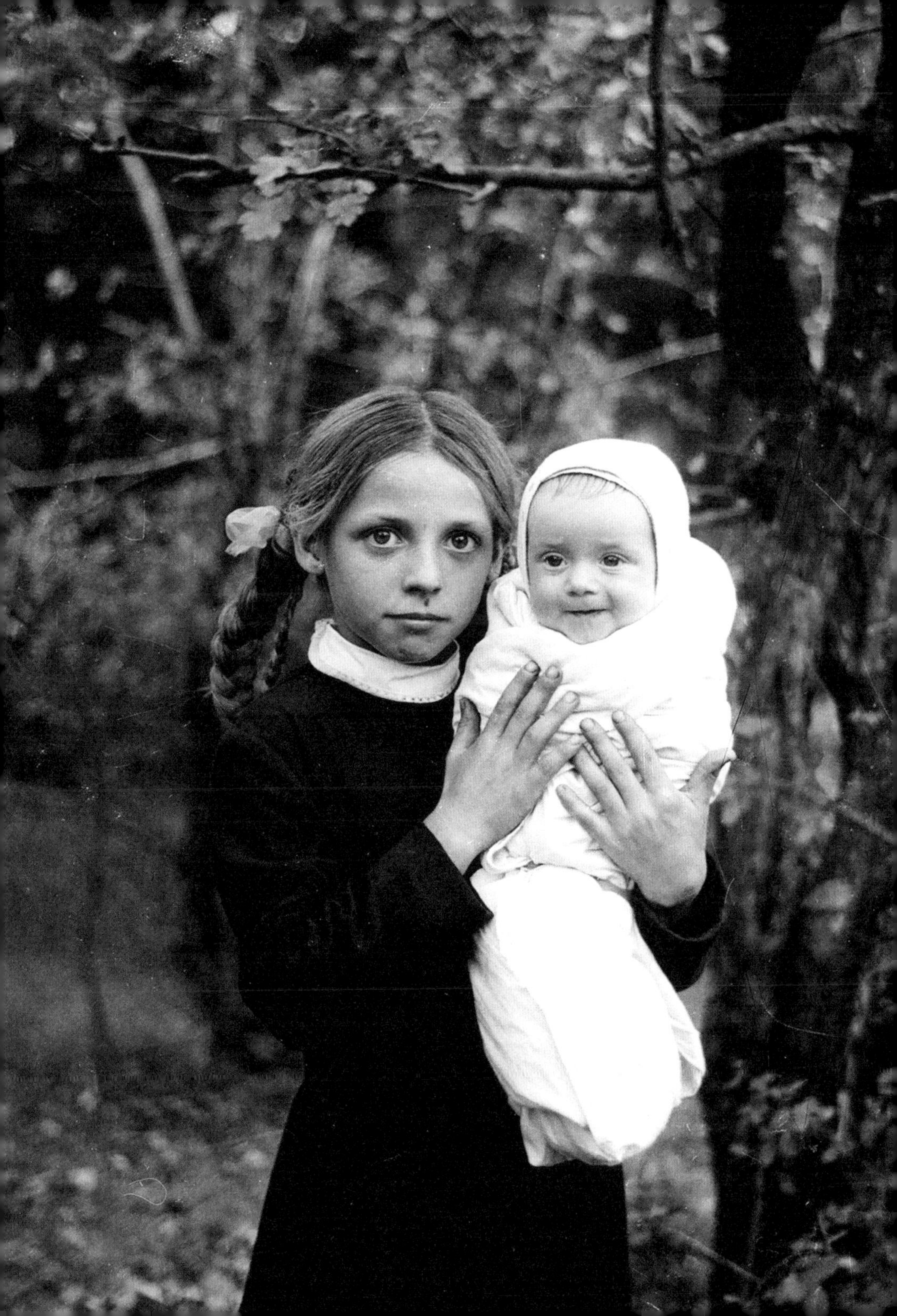

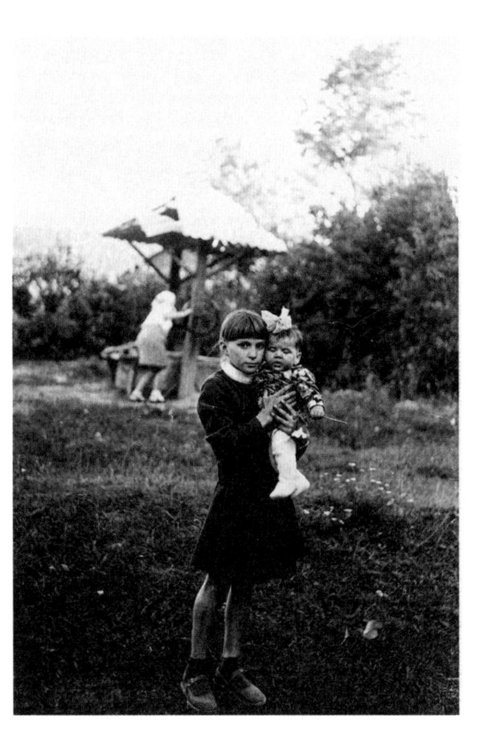

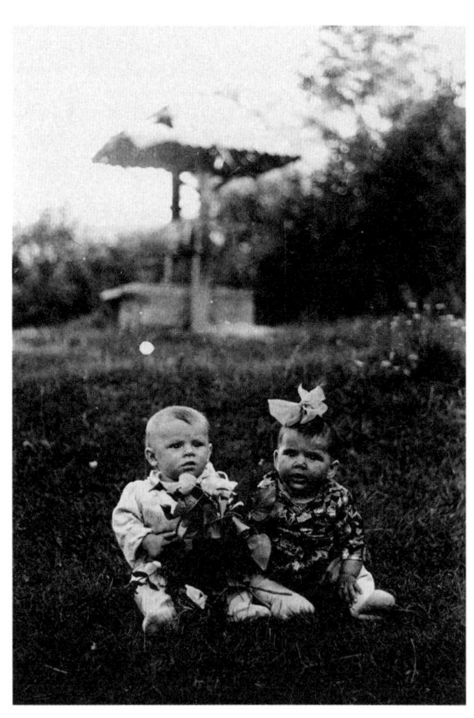

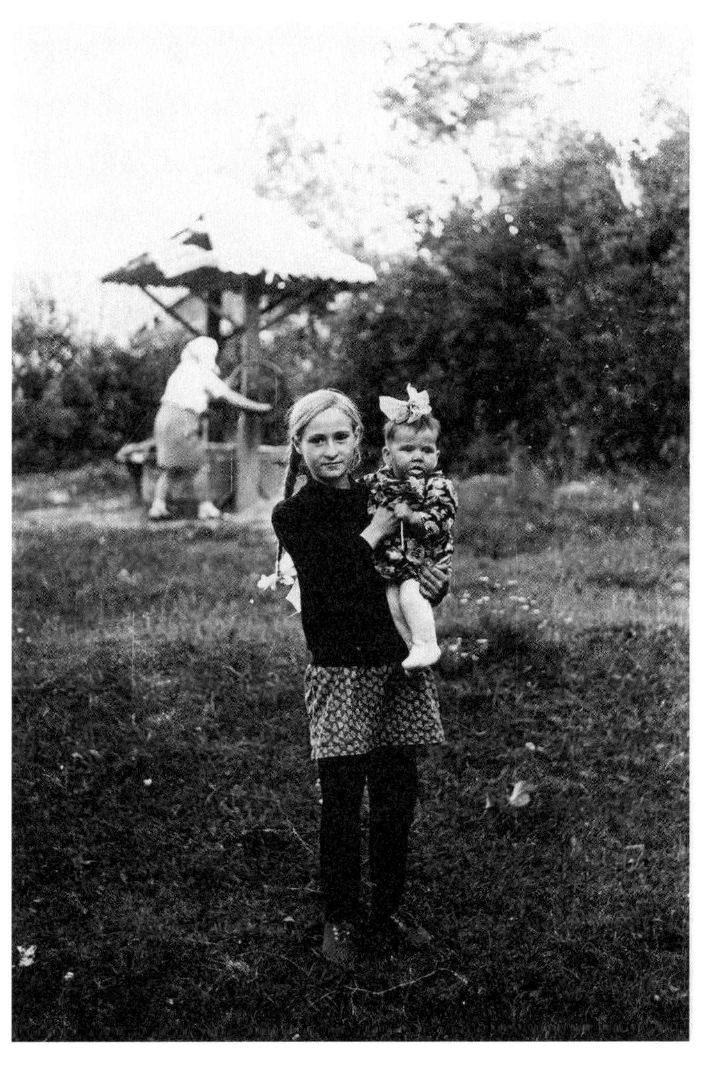

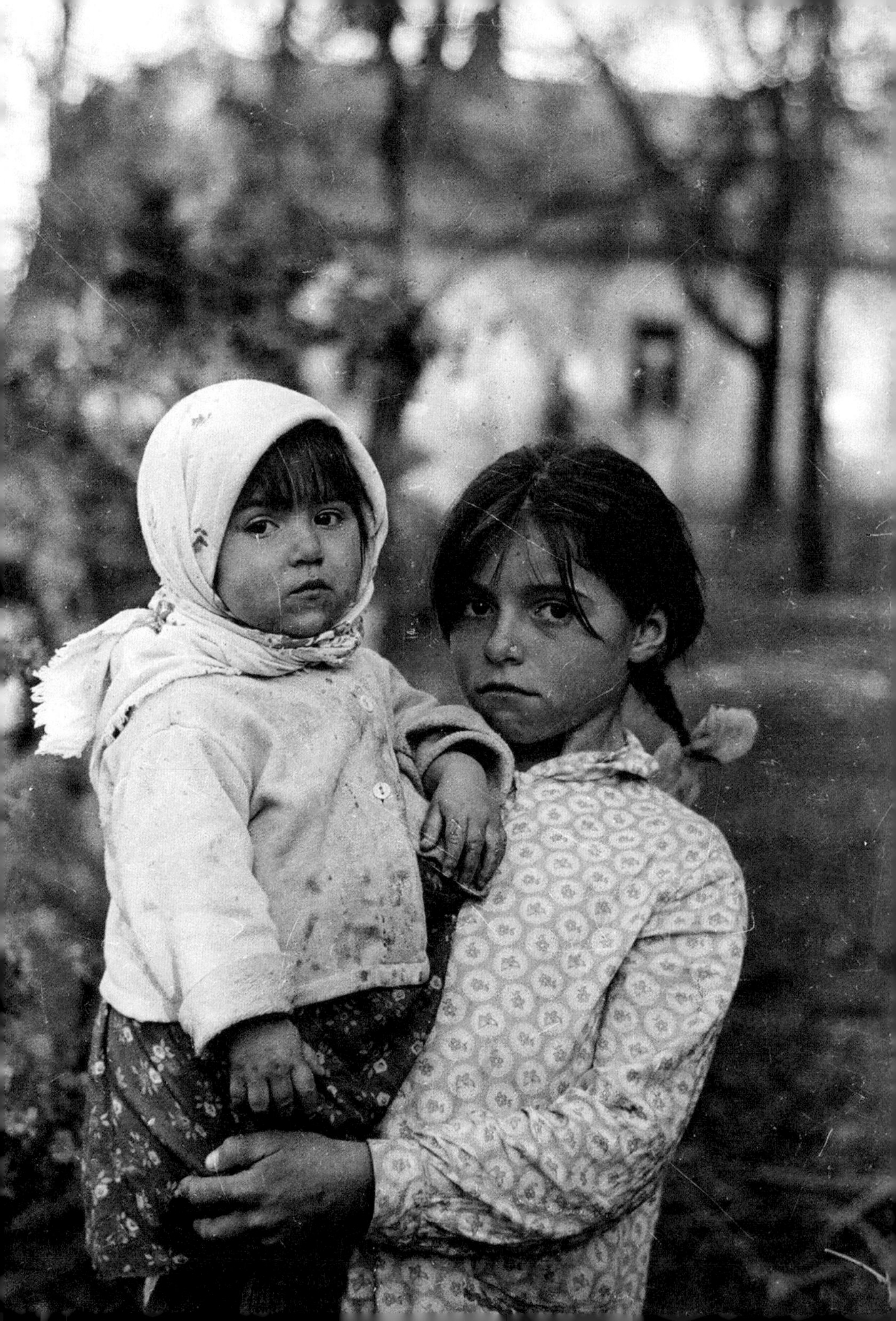

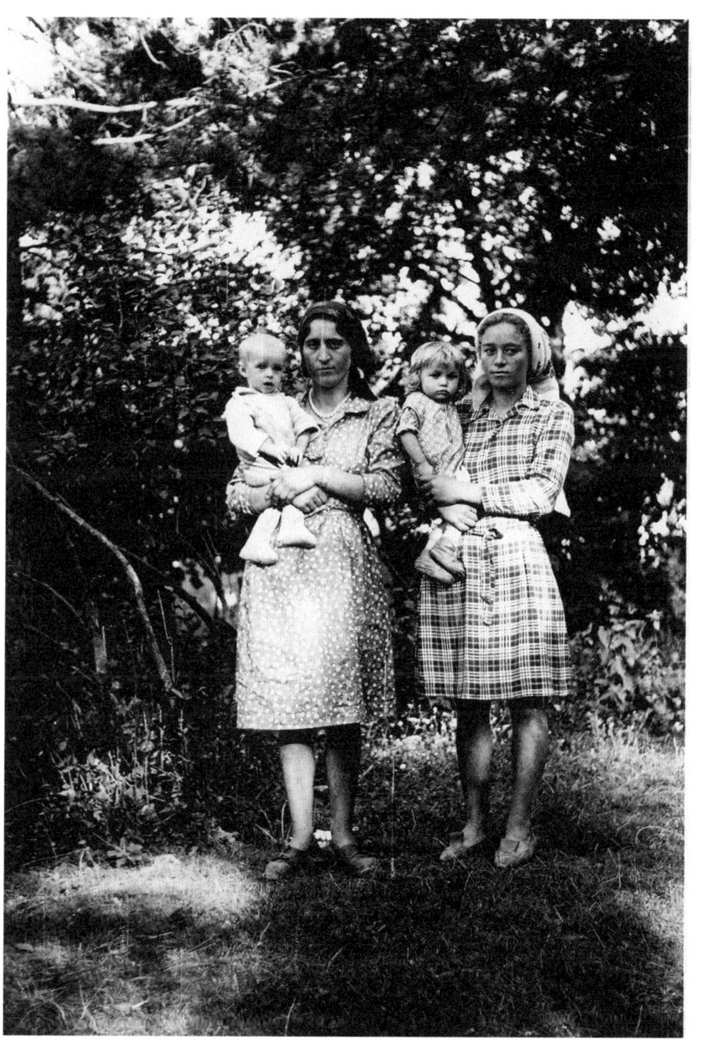

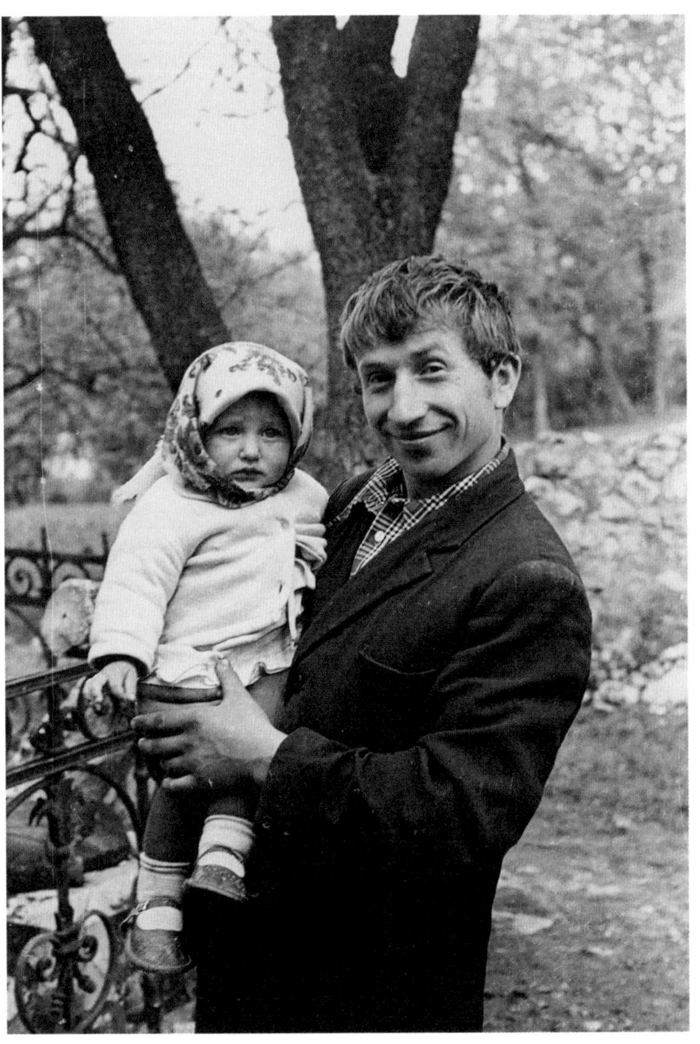

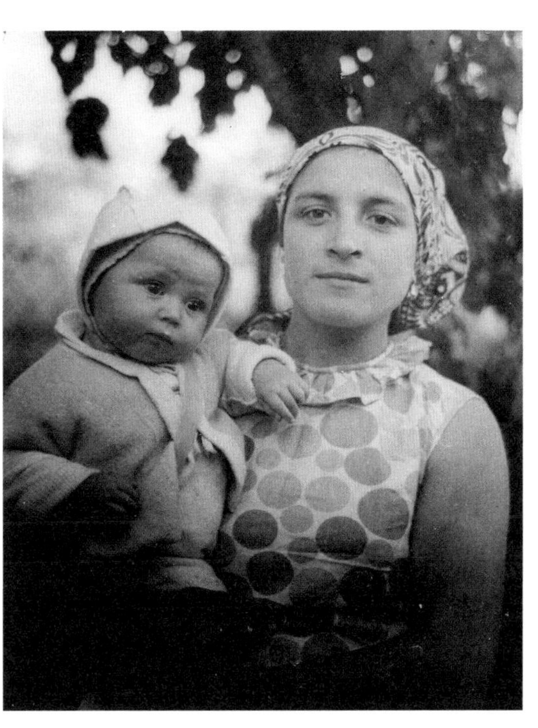

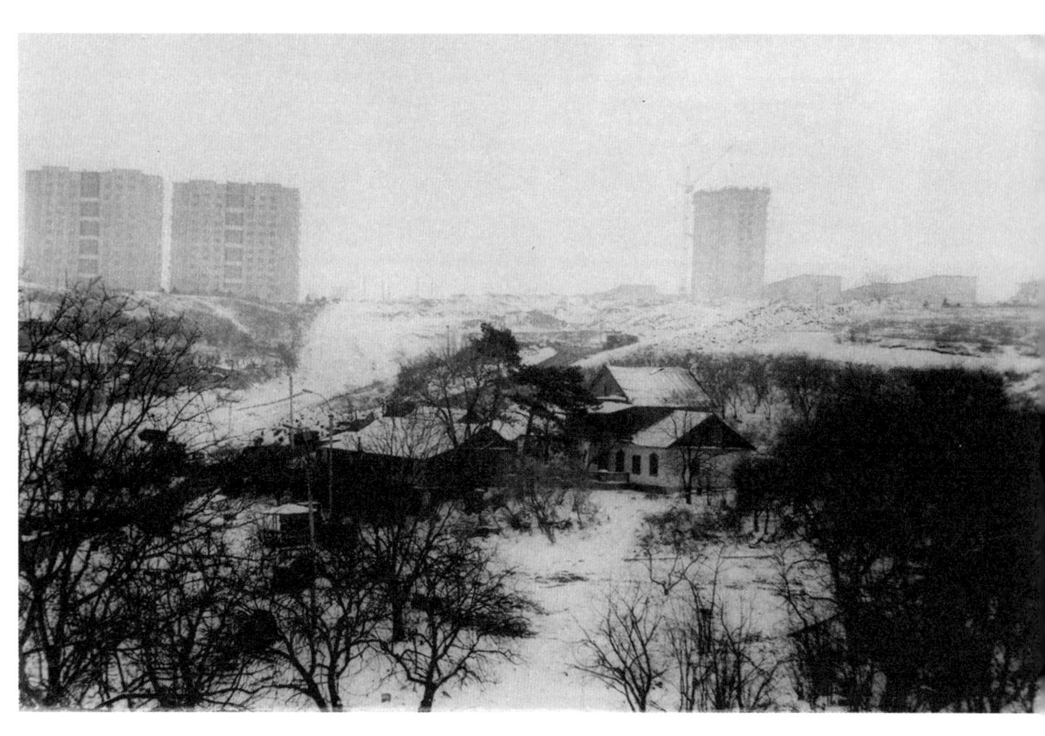

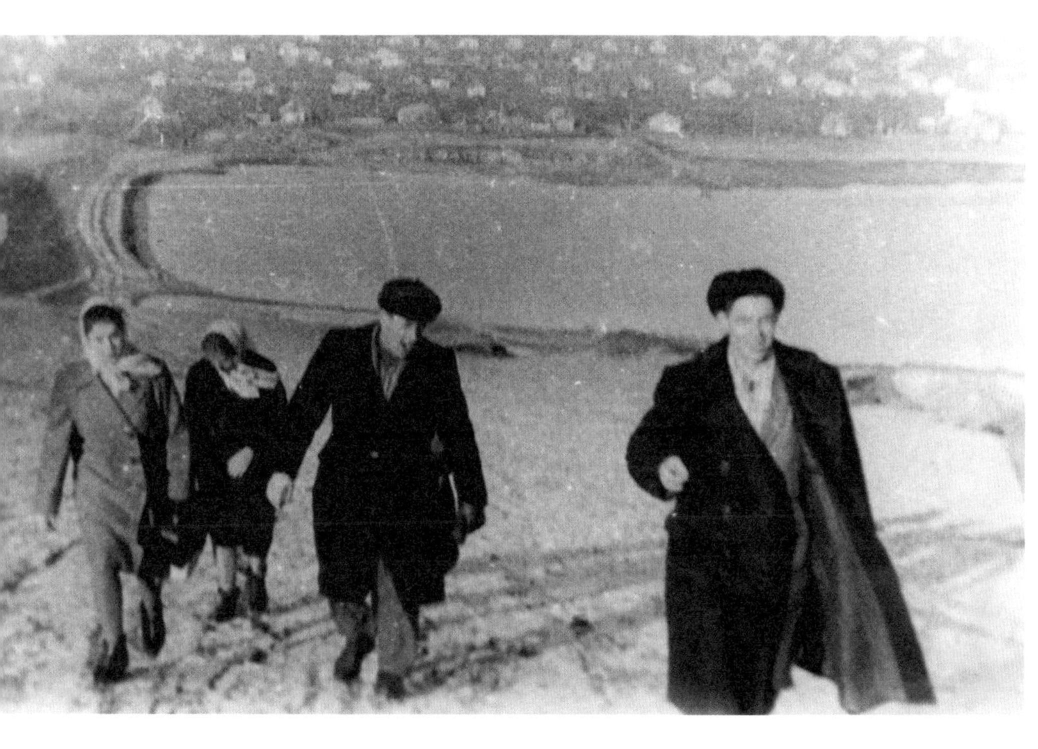

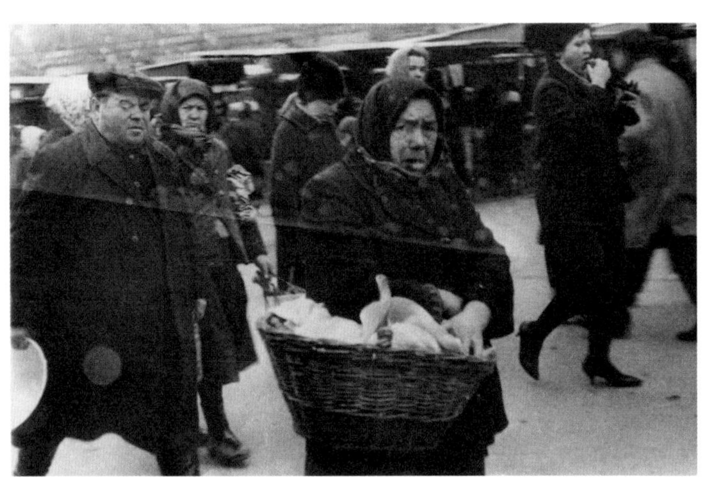

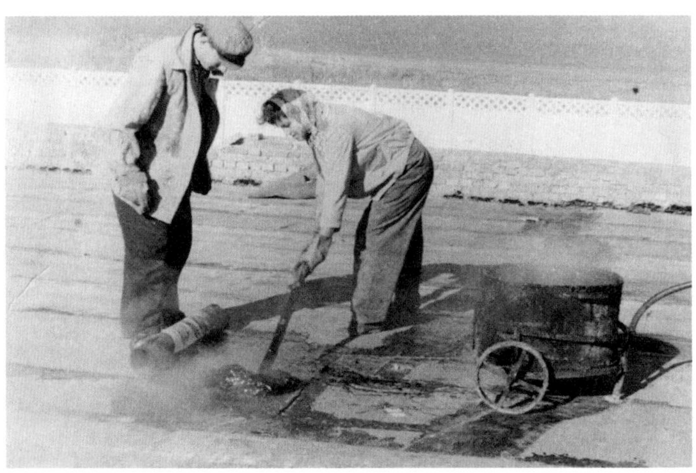

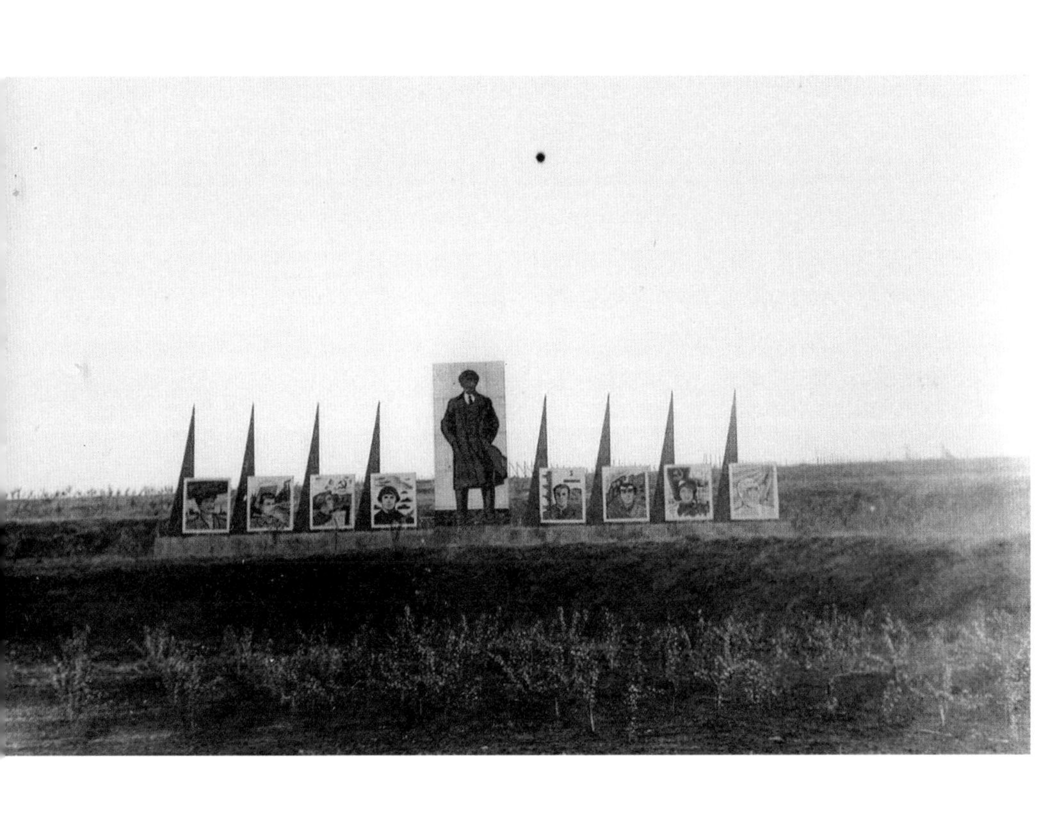

lost&found ist eine Buchreihe, in der verborgene oder verloren gegangene und wiederentdeckte Bildarchive vorgestellt werden. Sollten Sie ähnlich interessante Bilder kennen, melden Sie sich bei uns! Alle Bilder in dieser Publikation wurden nicht retuschiert.

lost&found is a book series which presents picture archives that were hidden or lost and and have been rediscovered. If you are aware of similarly interesting pictures, please get in touch with us! All pictures in this publication are unretouched.

Die Publikation erscheint anlässlich der Ausstellung/This booklet is published in conjunction with the exhibition:

»Die reine Leidenschaft – Amateurfotografien von Peter Dammann, Eugen Gerbert, Axel Herrmann und Vasilii Lefter«, Opelvillen Rüsselsheim, 2. Mai – 29. Juli 2018 / May 2–July 29, 2018
www.opelvillen.de

Herausgegeben von/Edited by Beate Kemfert, Markus Hartmann

Lektorat und Übersetzung/Copyediting and translation:
Hans Georg Hiller von Gaertringen, Tas Skorupa
Gestaltung/Design: Antonia Größchen
Druck und Bindung: Druckerei Ziegler, Neckarbischofsheim
Produktion, Konzept, Verlag/Production, concept, publisher:
Hartmann Books, Rulfinger Straße 18, 70567 Stuttgart, Germany
www.hartmannprojects.com

Erste Auflage/First Edition: April 2018
Band/Volume: 2
ISBN 978-3-96070-023-4

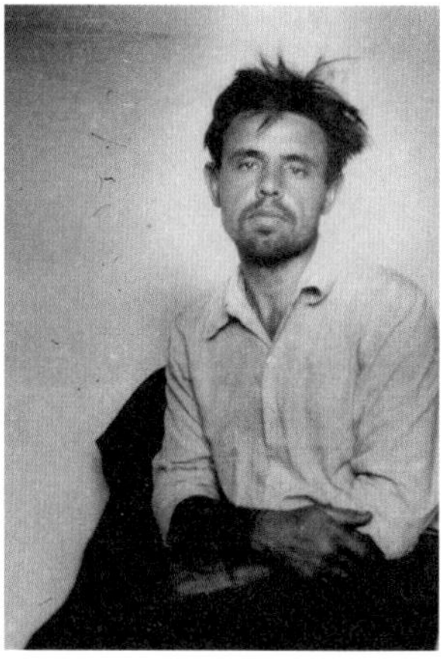

Mit freundlicher Unterstützung von/
With generous support from

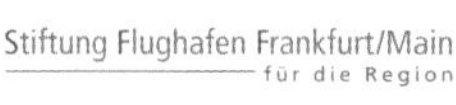

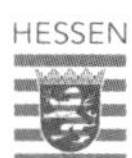